What is Mandala?

The Mandala word from Sanskrit. 'Man' represents the 'Mind' and 'da' represents 'Maintenance'. The essence of the word meaning everything is completed within the mind.

Mandala is a circular figure. The circle represents the universe symbolizing unity and harmony. Colouring mandalas can help a person spiritually, emotionally, and mentally.

By colouring Mandalas you express yourself comfortably and mindfully. The activity brings calmness, reduces stress levels and aids in creating a better version of you. It is a form of effective brain exercise. Colouring these uses the creative side of your brain.

Your true self can be found by colouring these Mandala.

Namaste!
Jey

BE CREATIVE & BE IMAGINATIVE

Copyright © 2017 Authentikminds. All rights reserved.

Meditate through Mandala Hand Drawn Colouring Book Creative Art Therapy by Jey

Artist Full Name : Jeyanthi Ramamoorthy

Artist Website : www.Authentikminds.com

ISBN-13: 978-1974178643

Mandalas to Colour

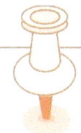

1. Authentic
2. Wholeness
3. Kindness
4. Endurance
5. Permanence
6. Divinity
7. Unity
8. Power
9. Healing
10. Passion
11. Wisdom
12. Reflection
13. Transformation
14. Vivid
15. Vibrant
16. Consciousness
17. Truthful
18. Imagination
19. Vision
20. Innovation
21. Compassion
22. Forbearance
23. Gratification
24. Satisfaction
25. Gentleness

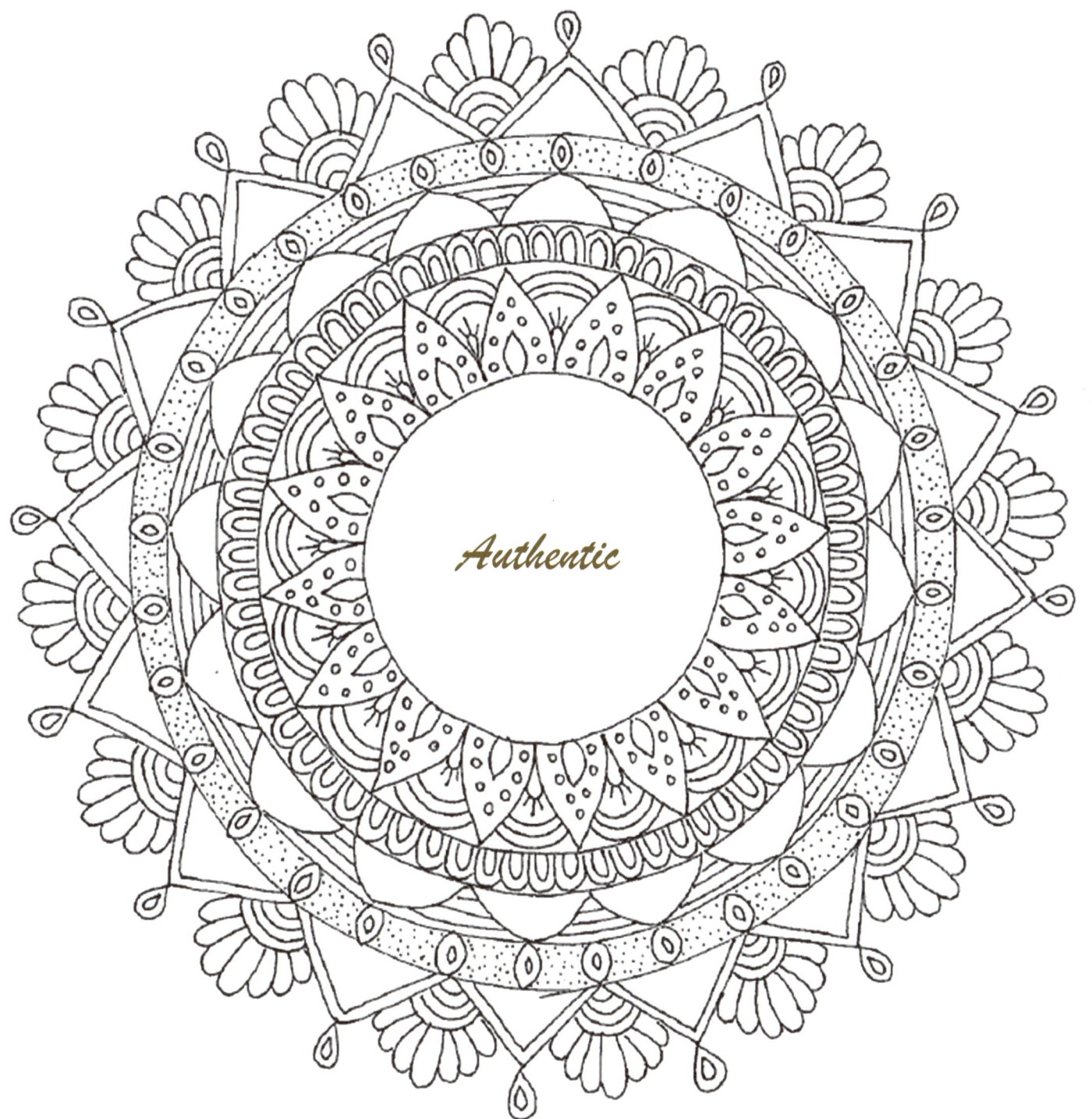

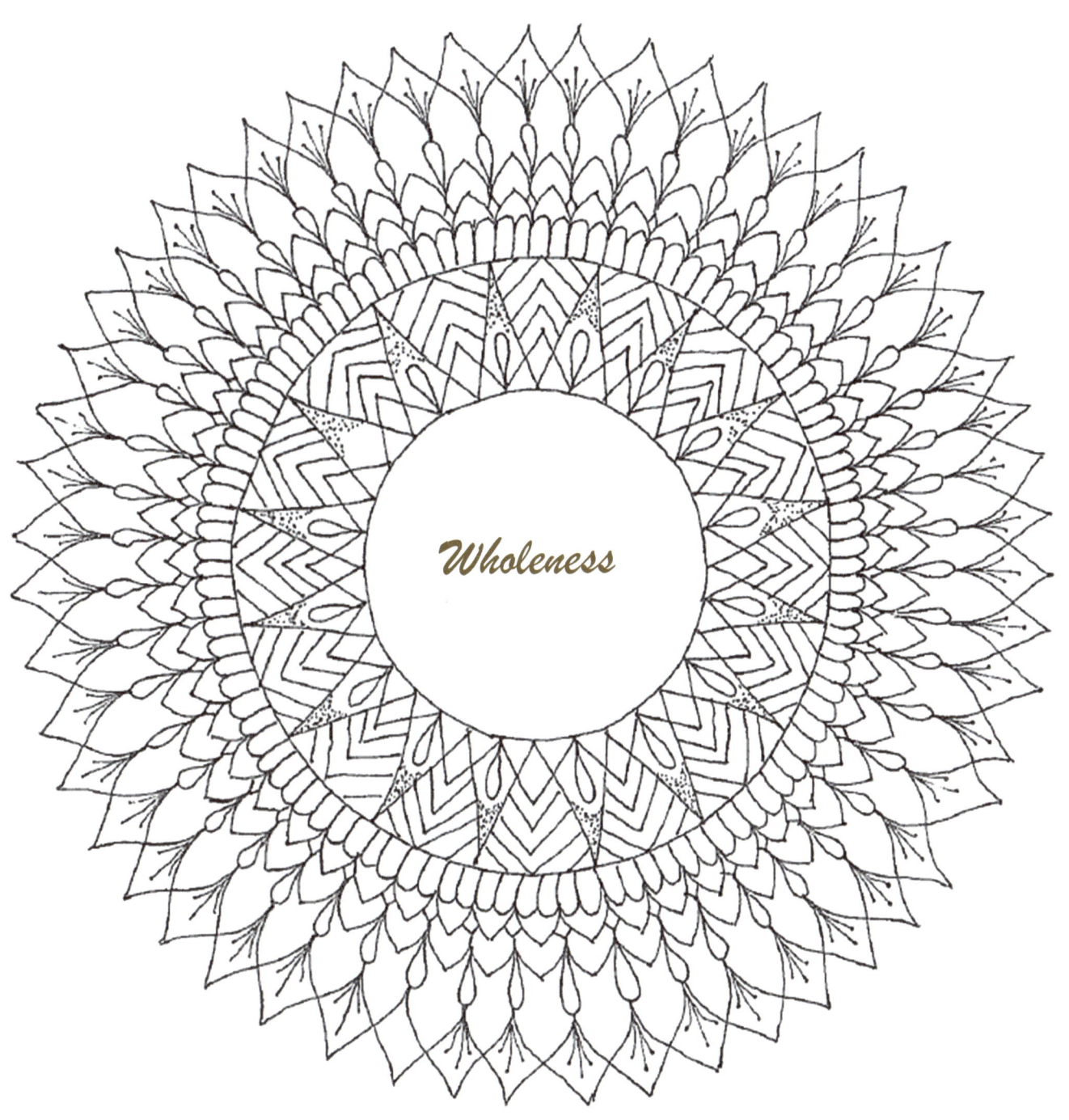

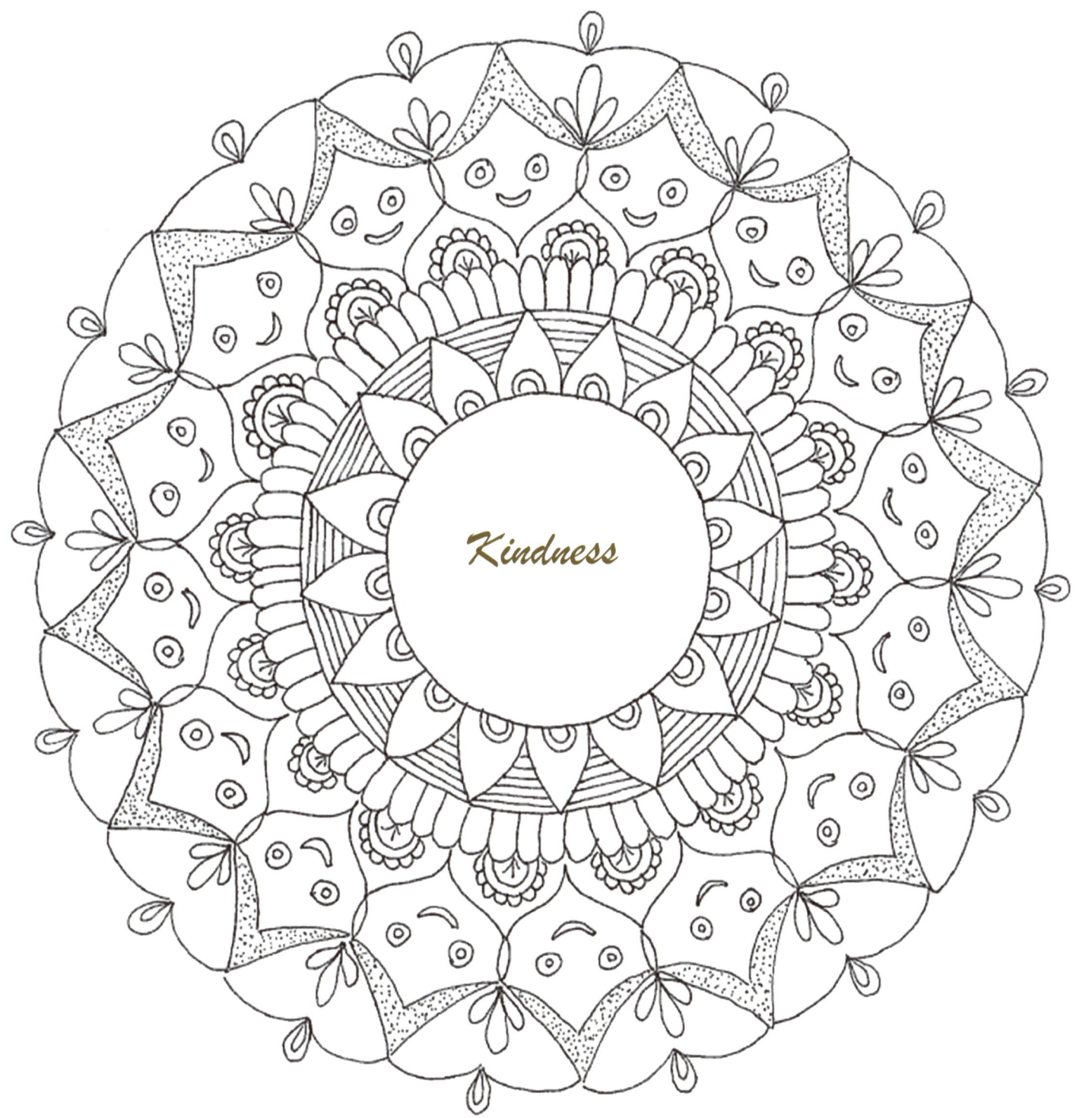

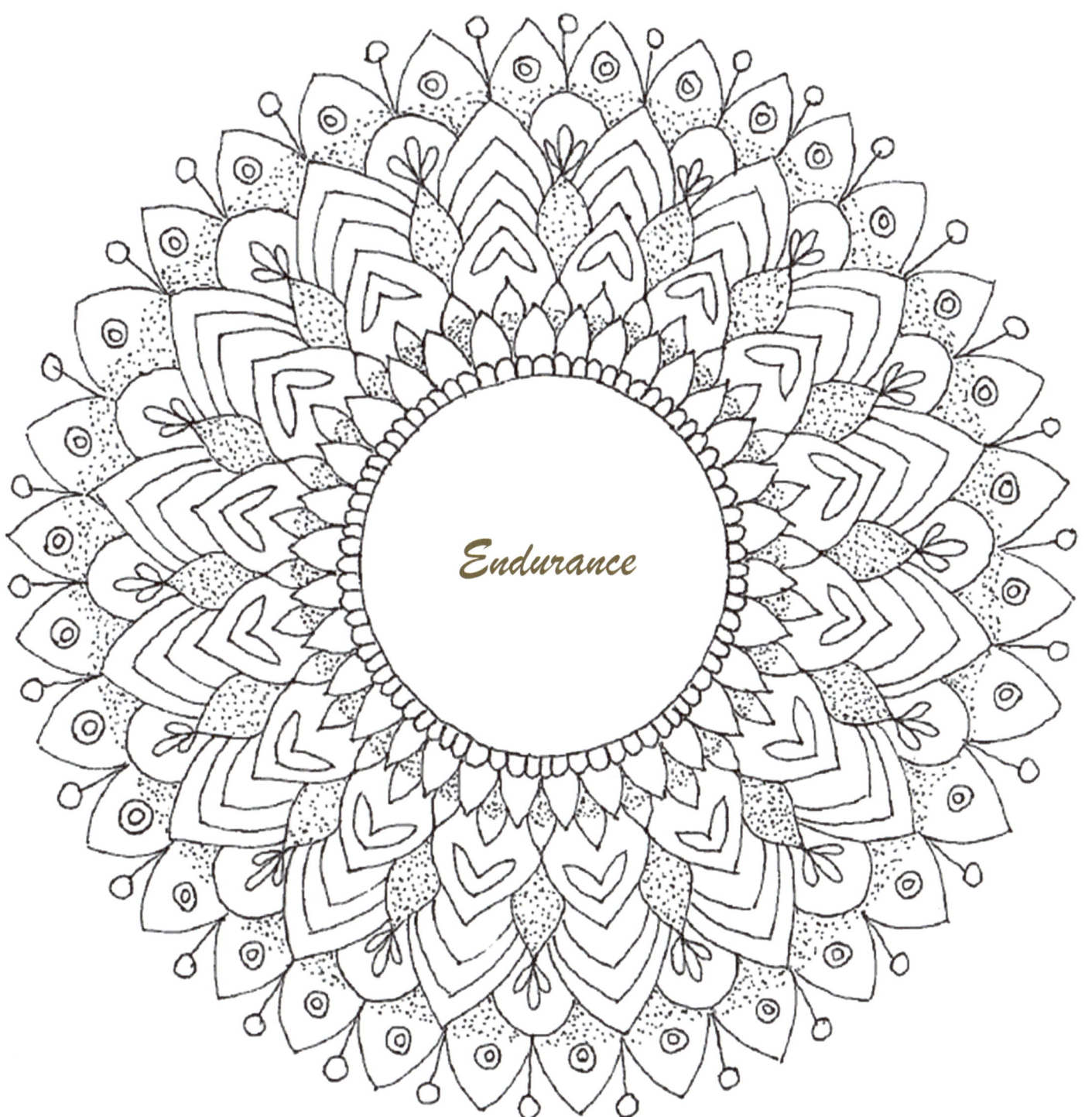

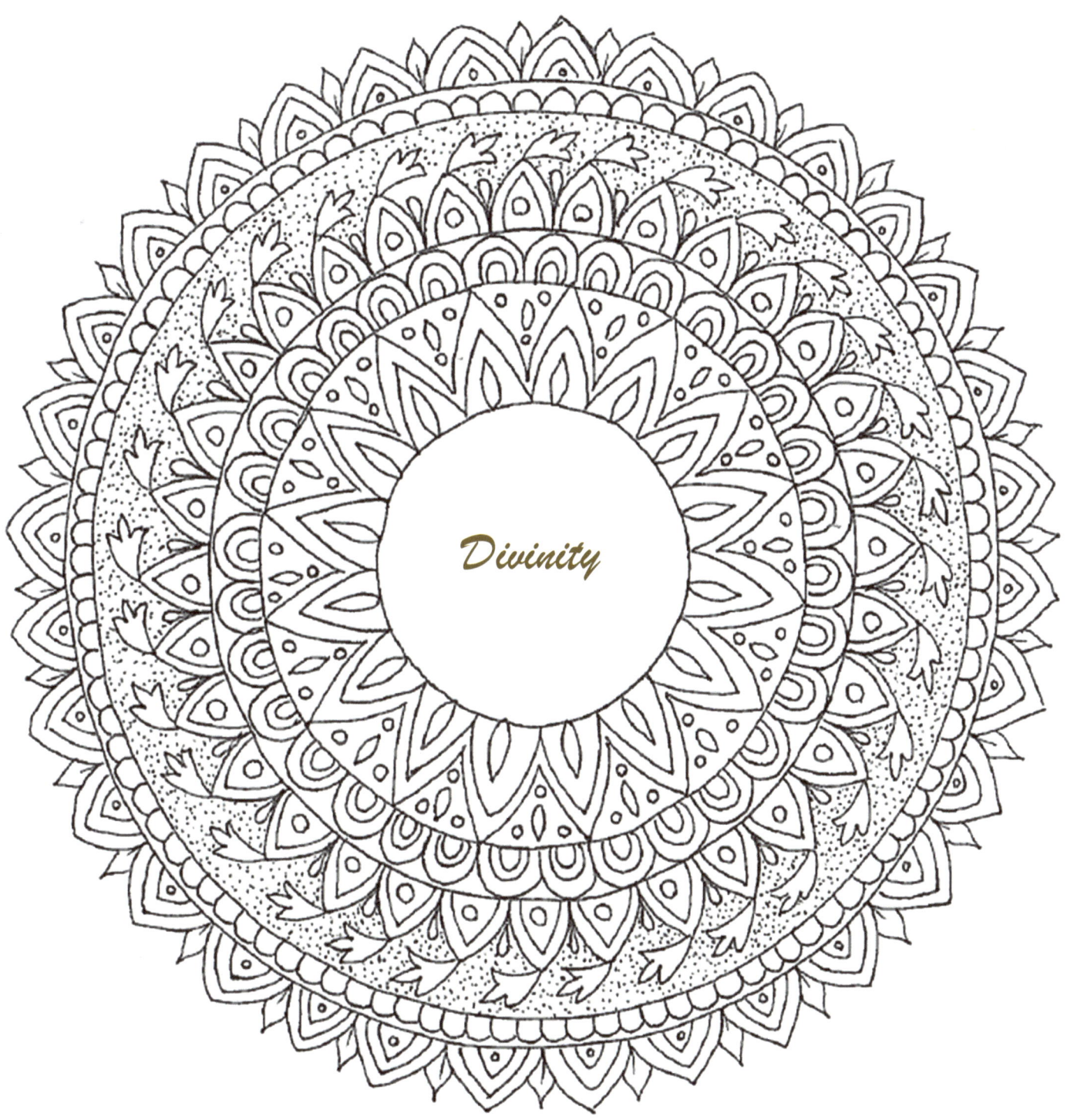

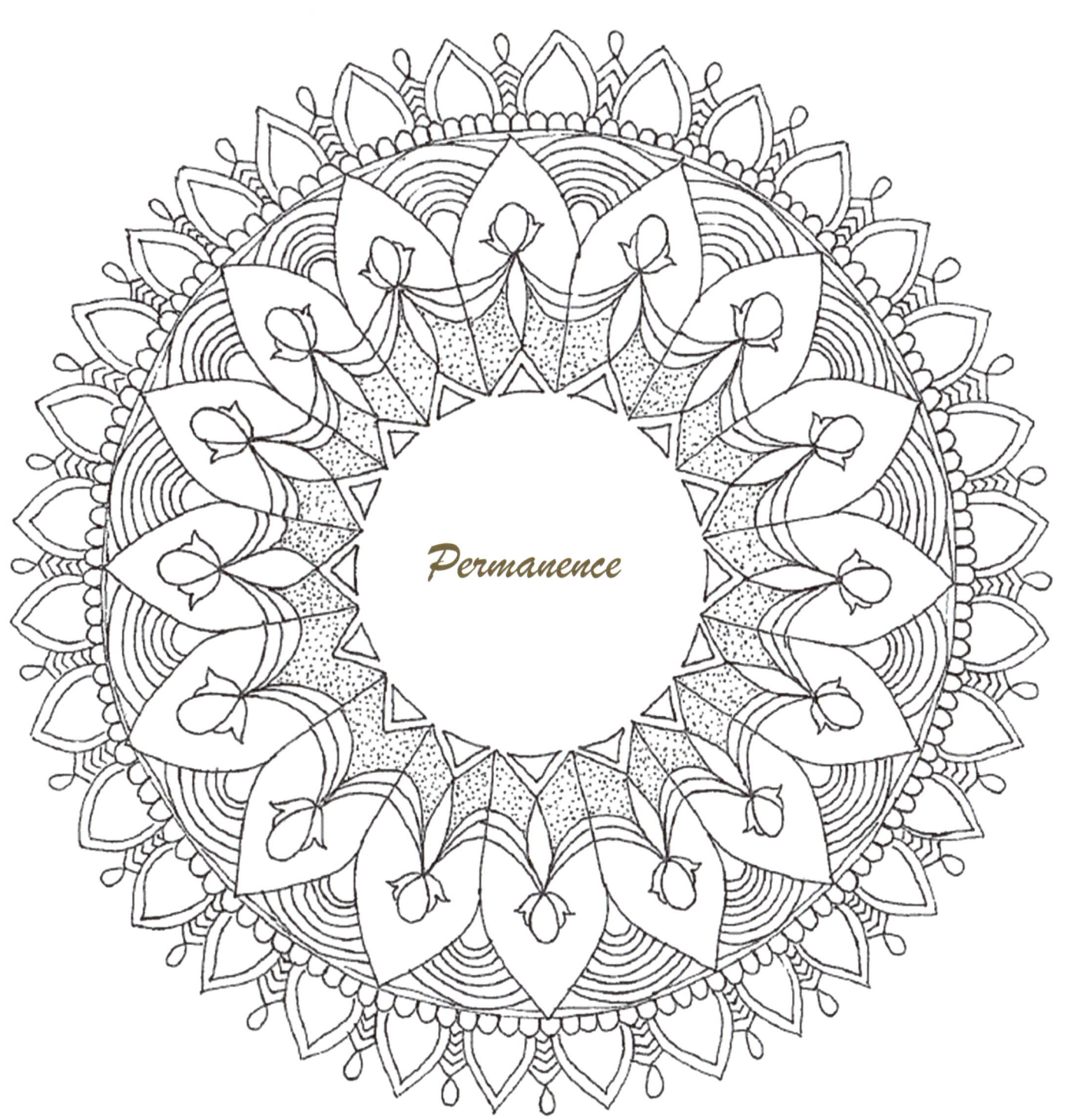

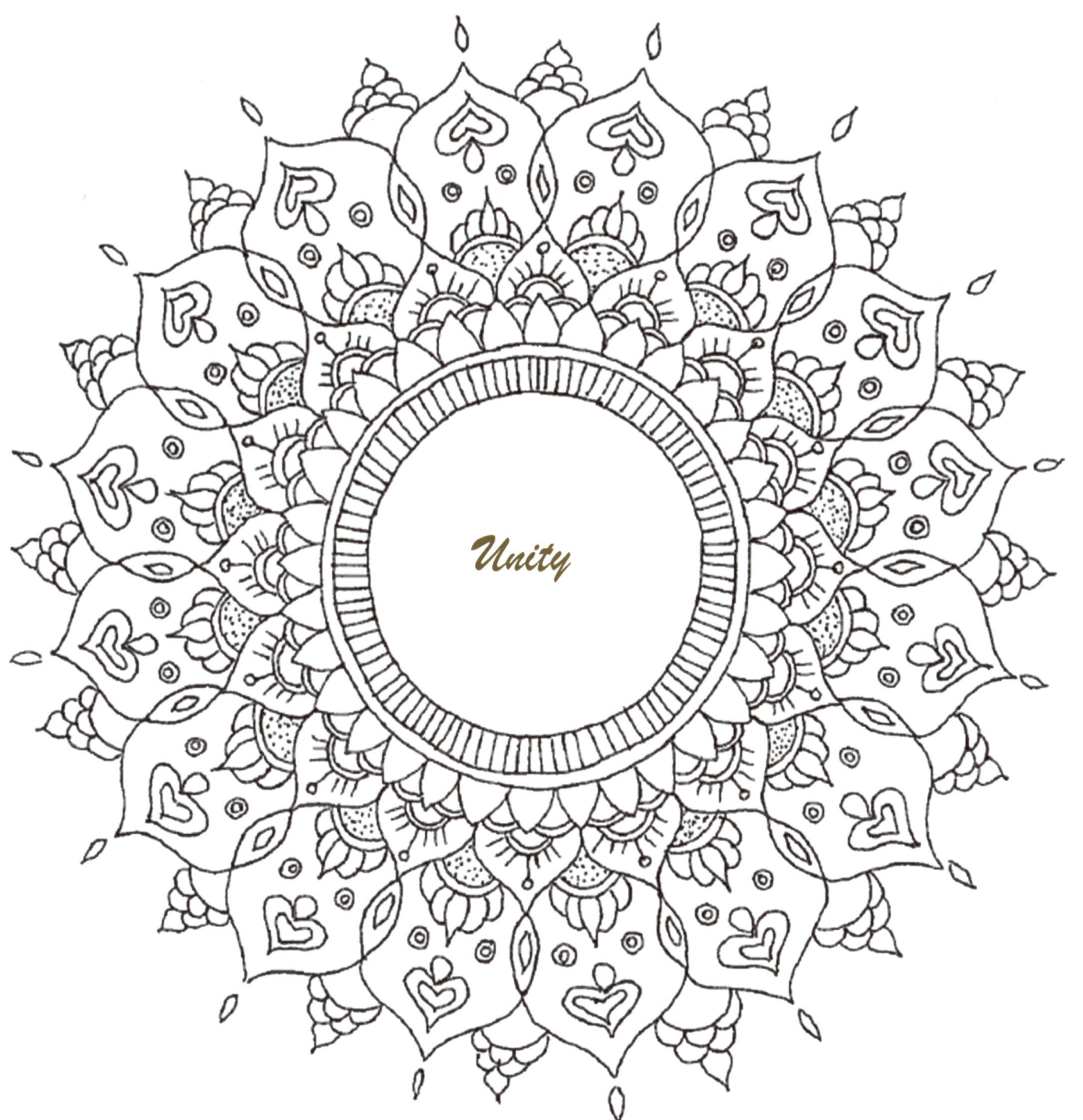

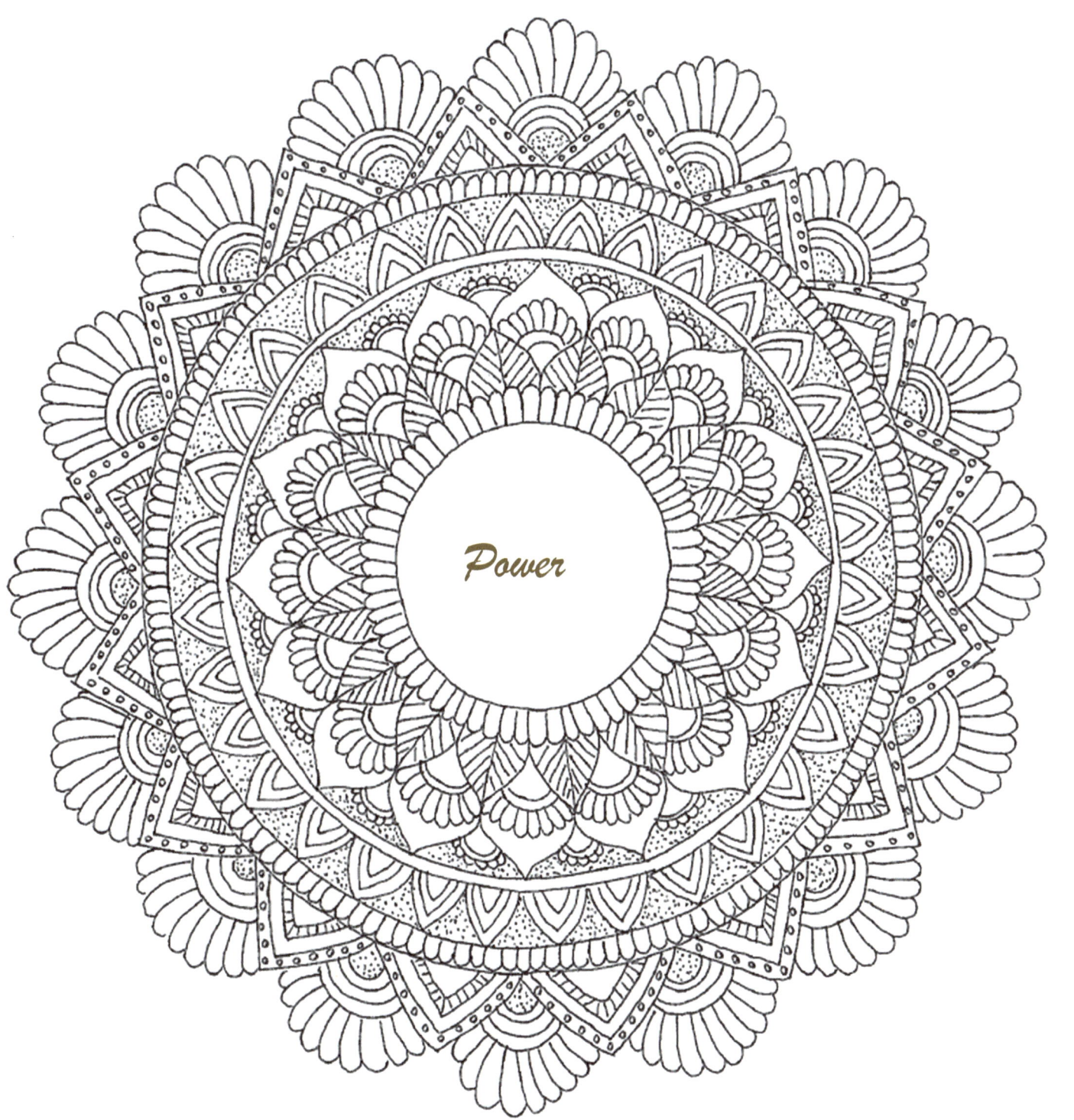

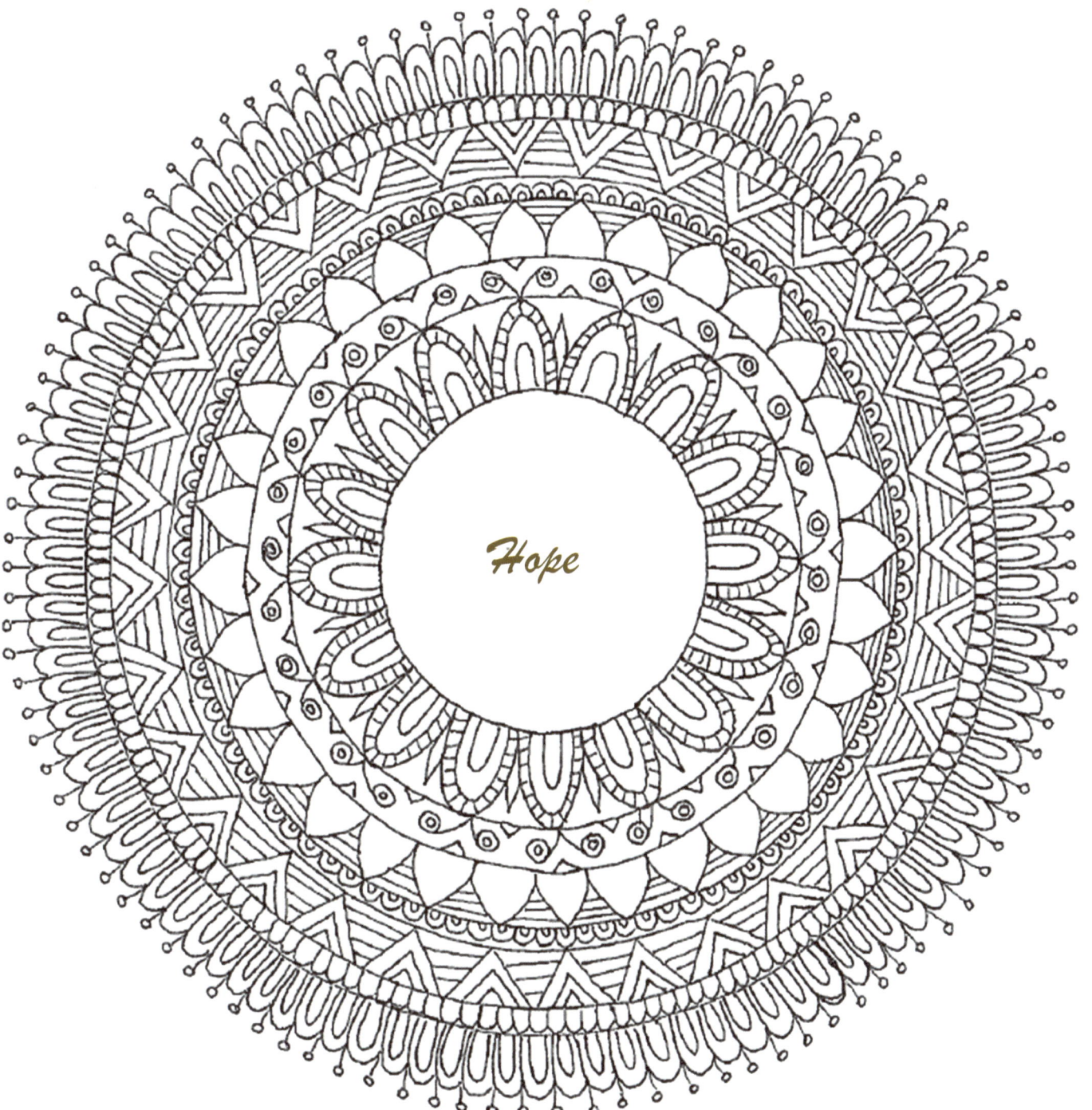

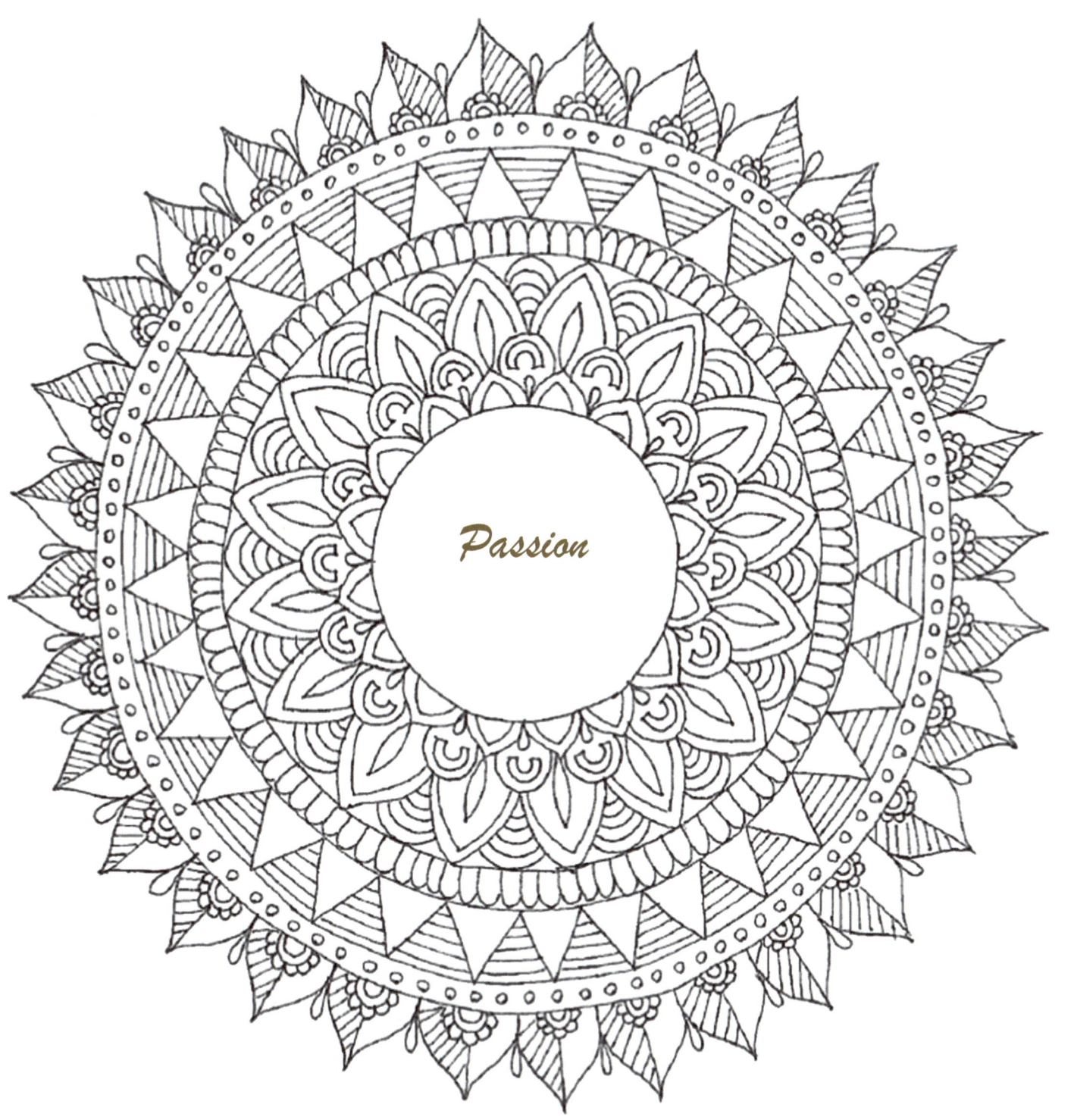

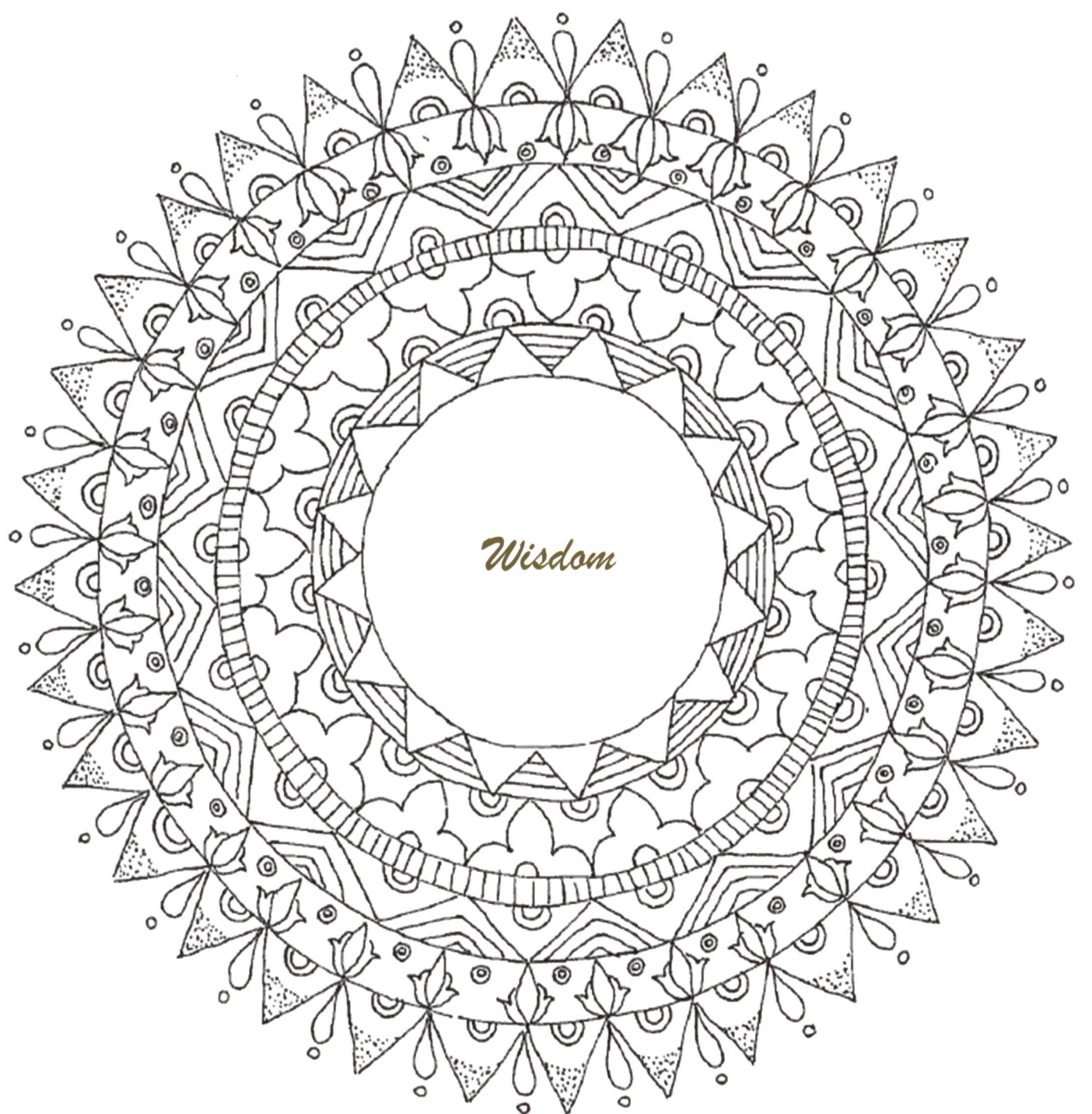

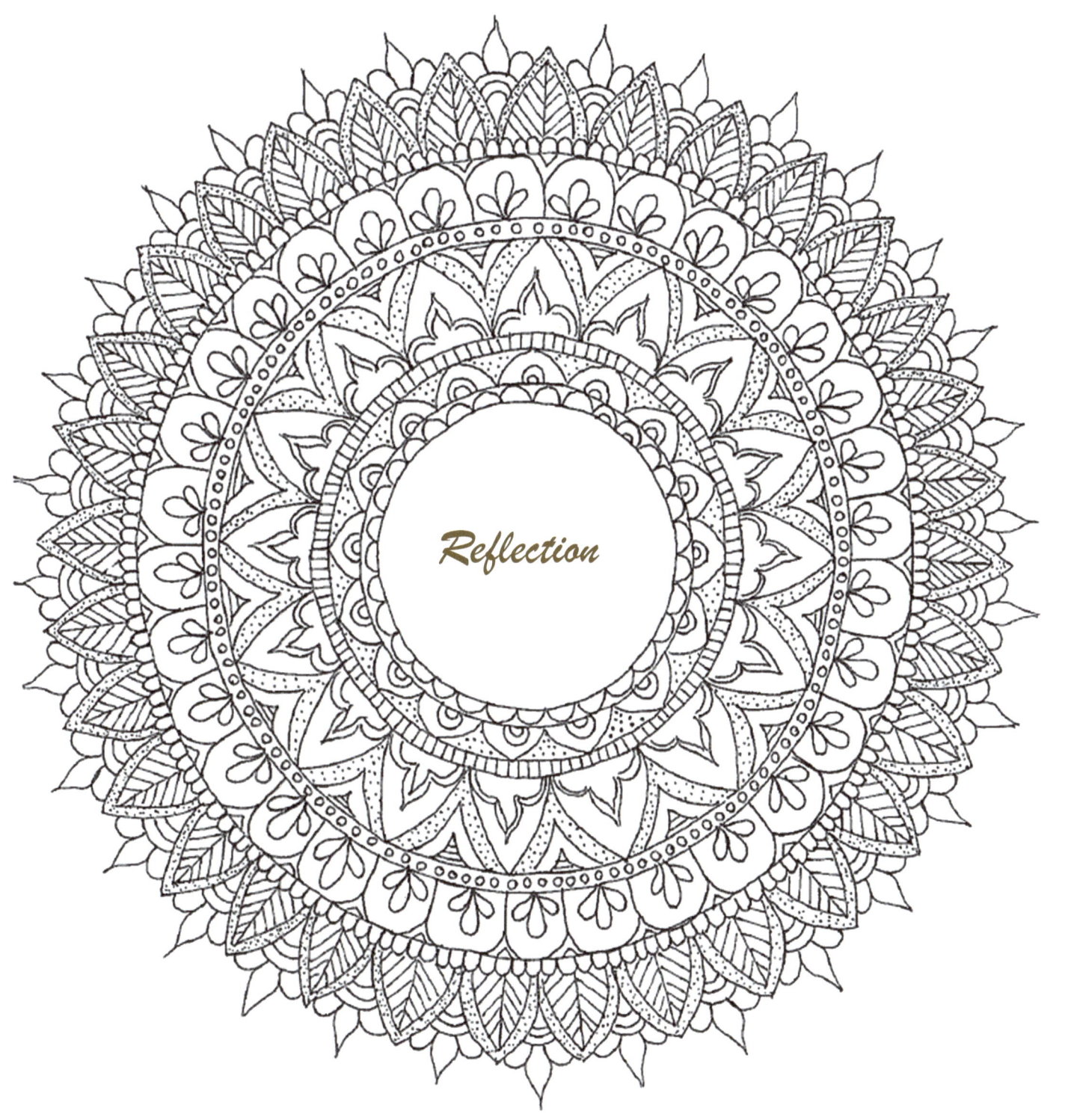

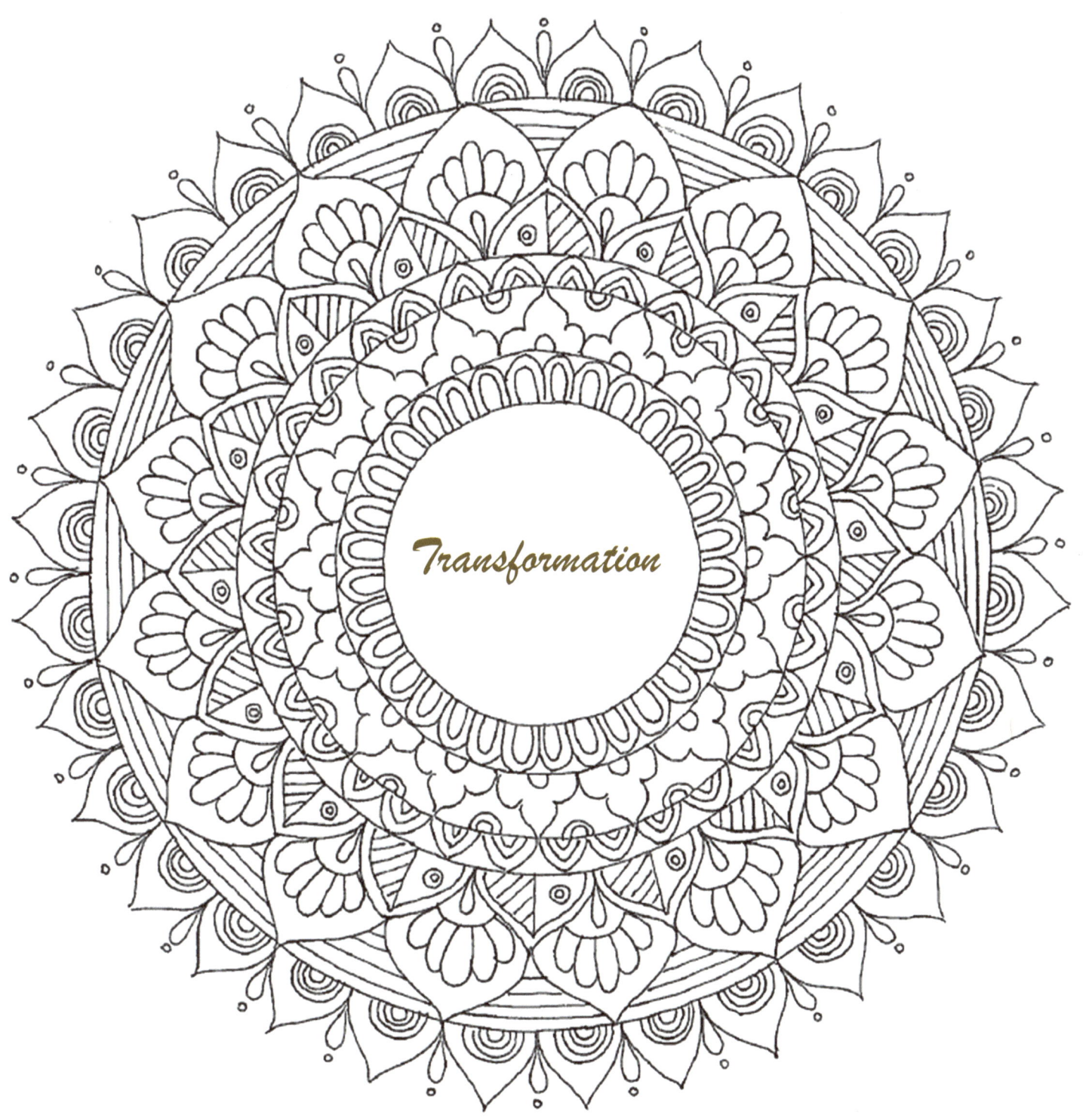

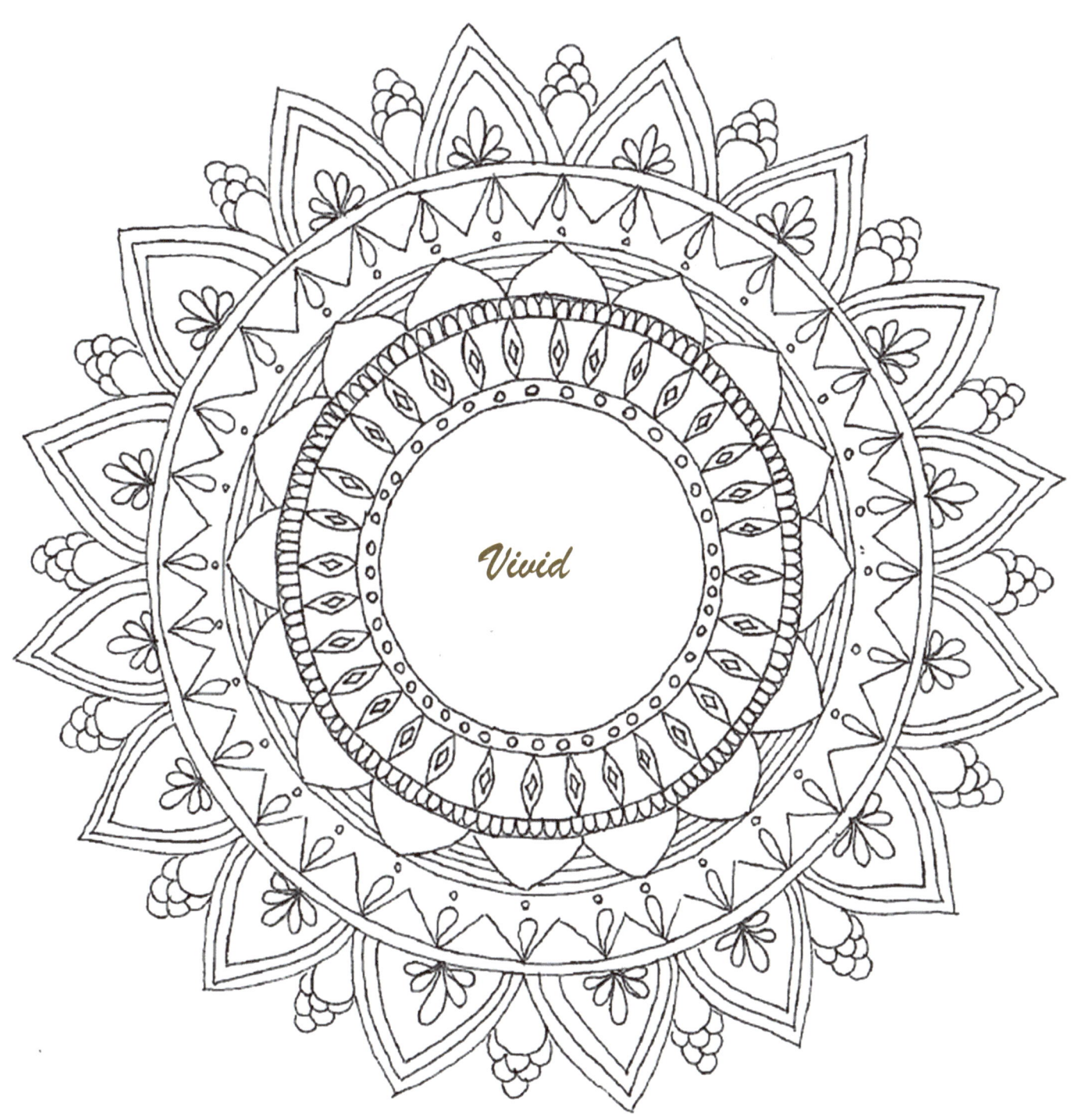

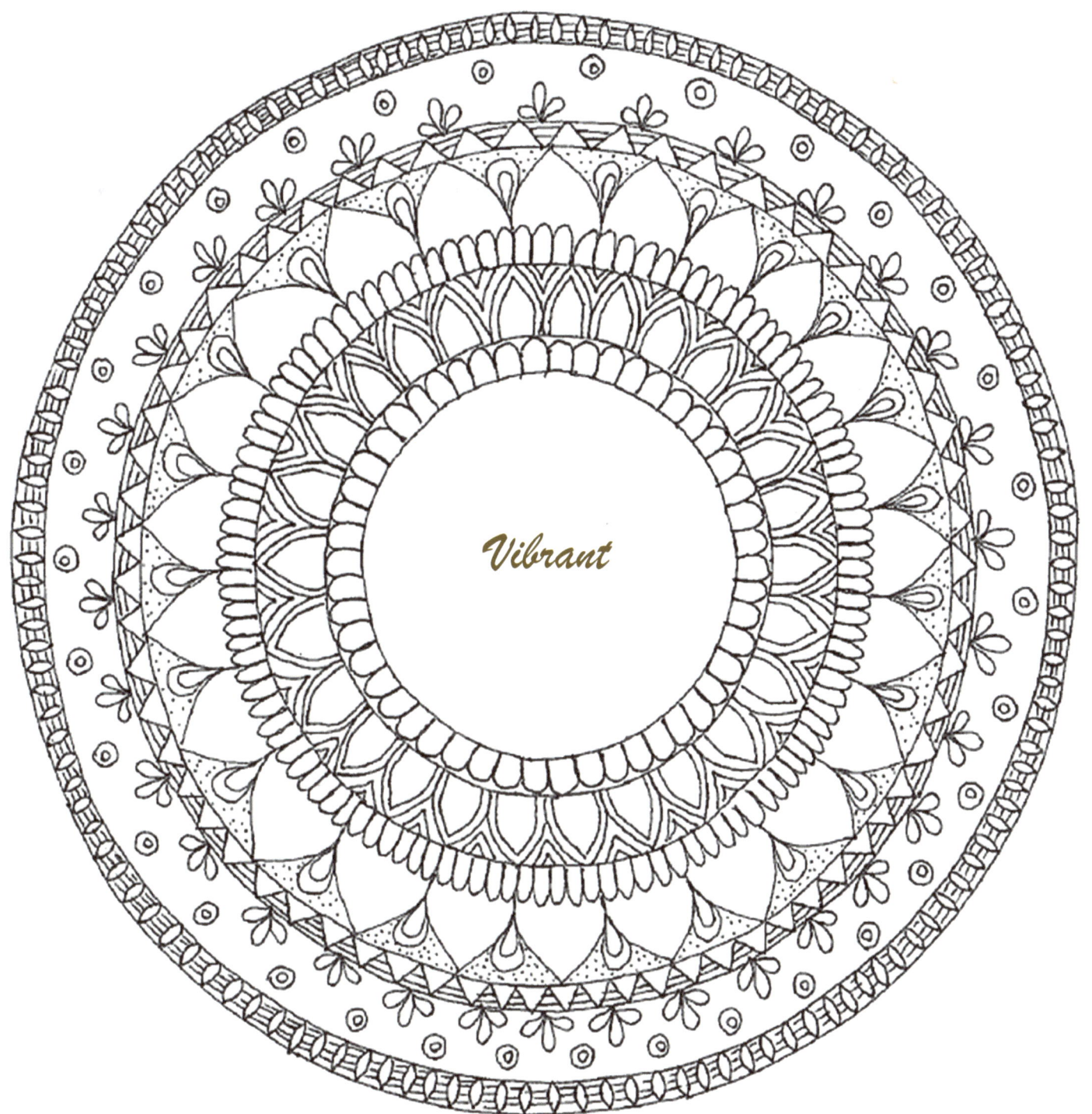

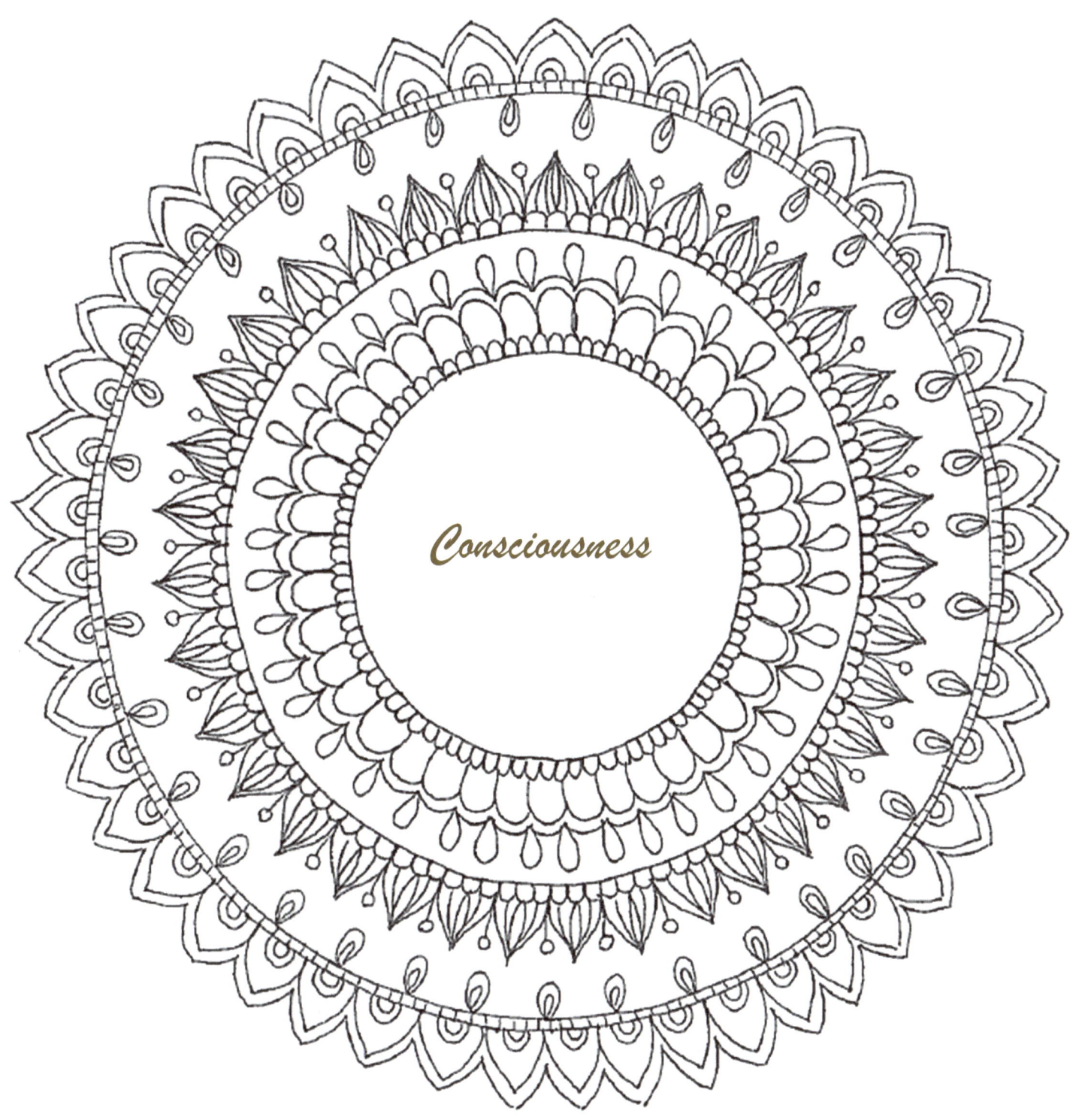

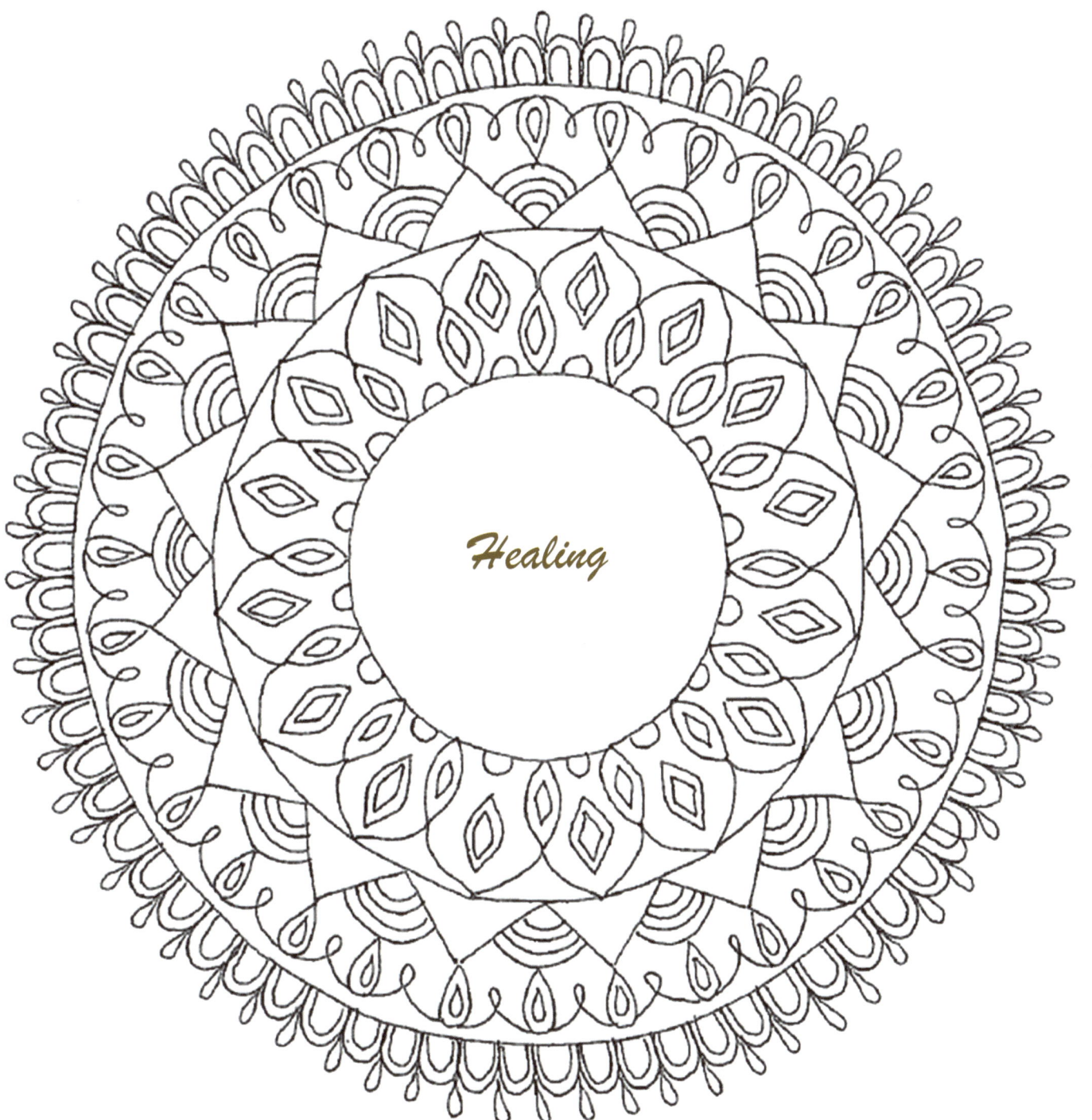

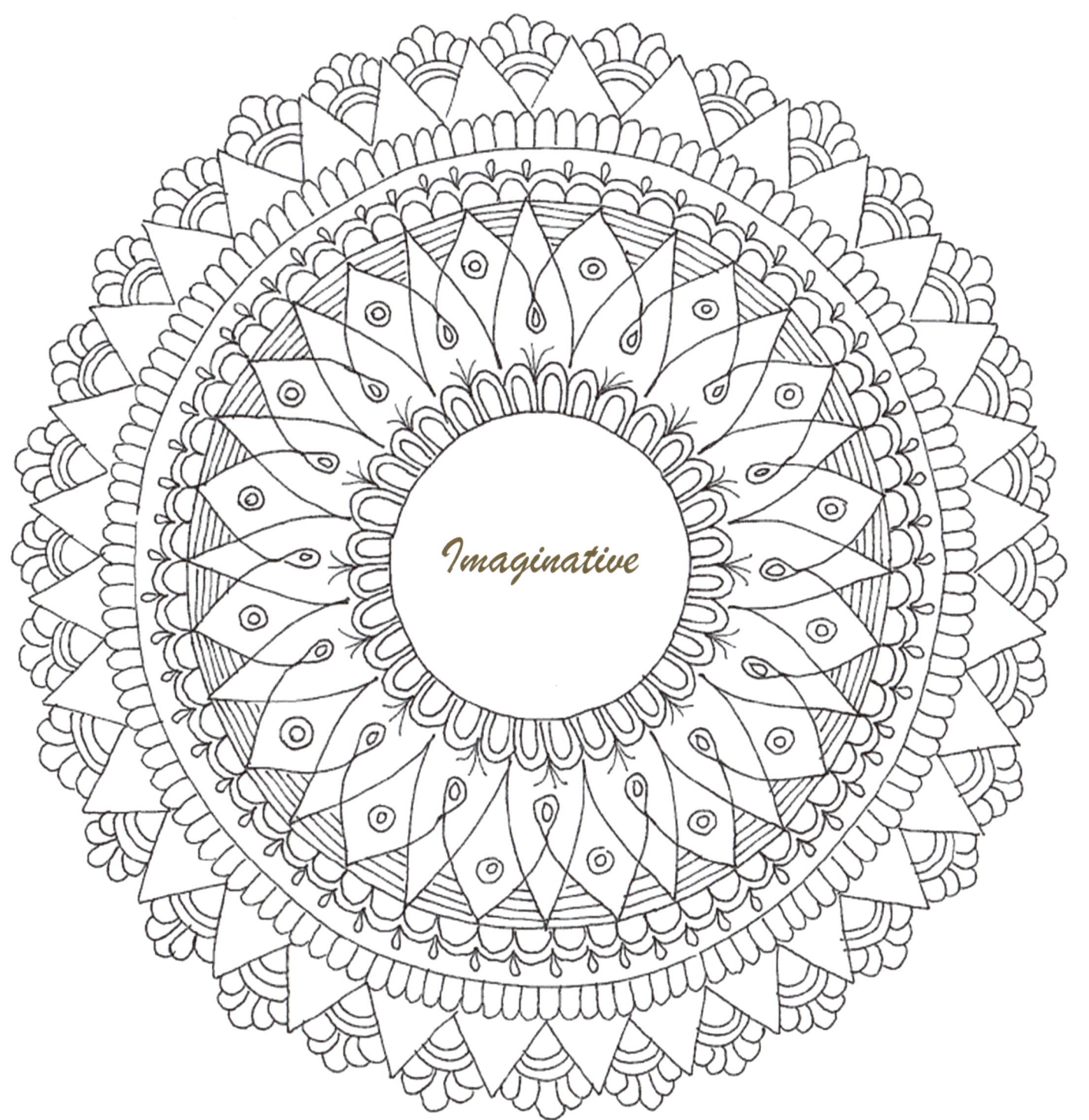

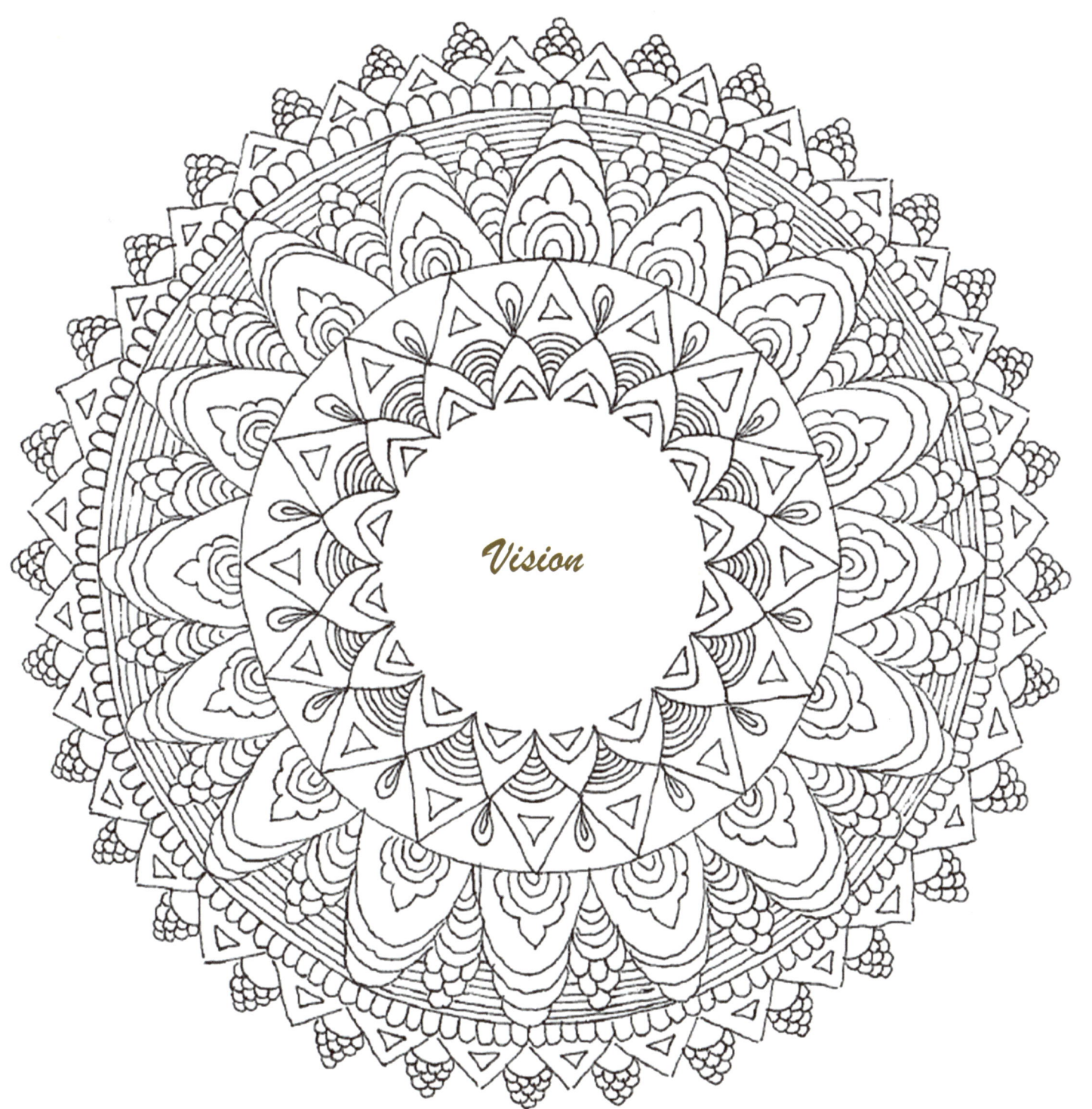

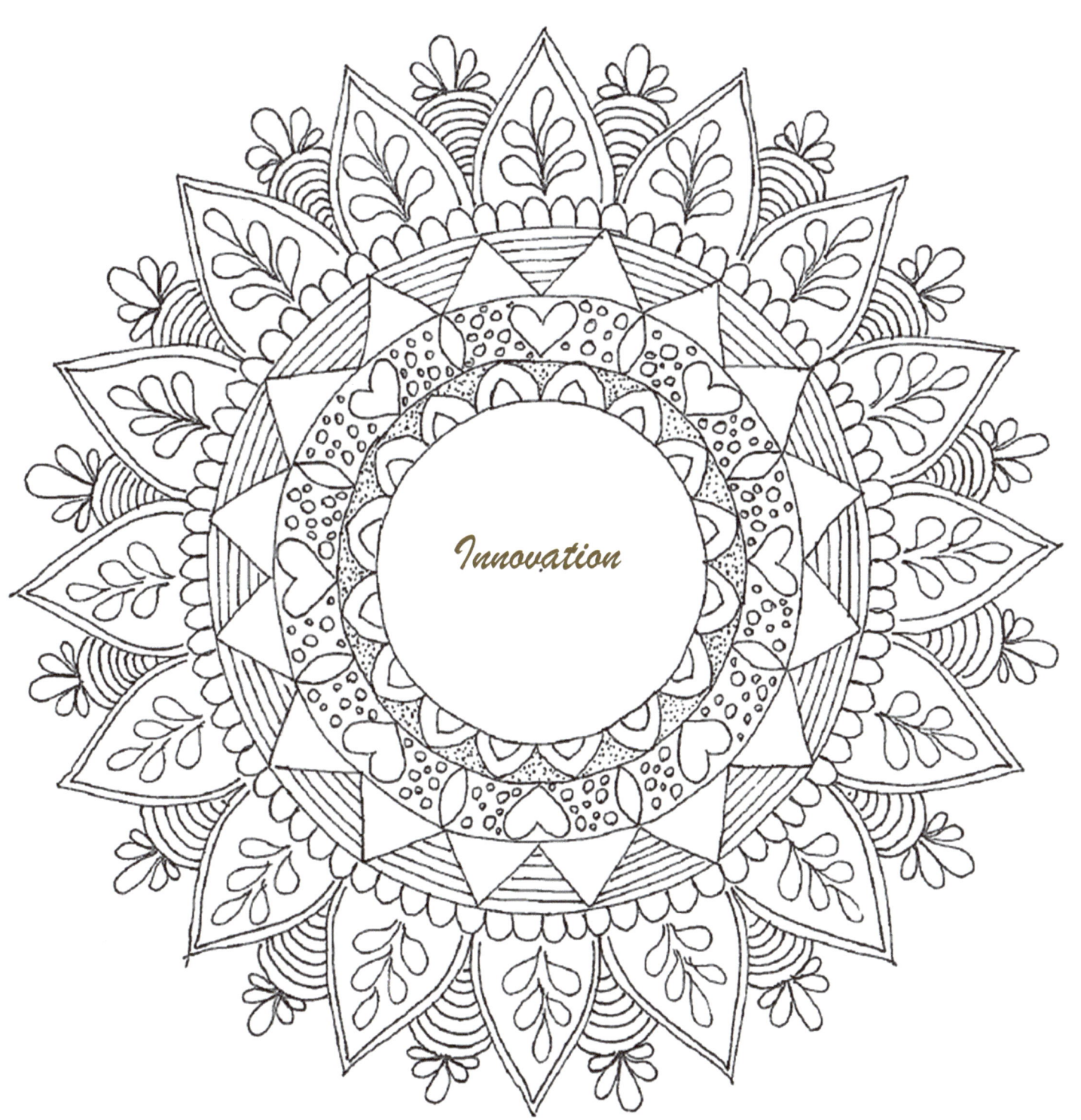

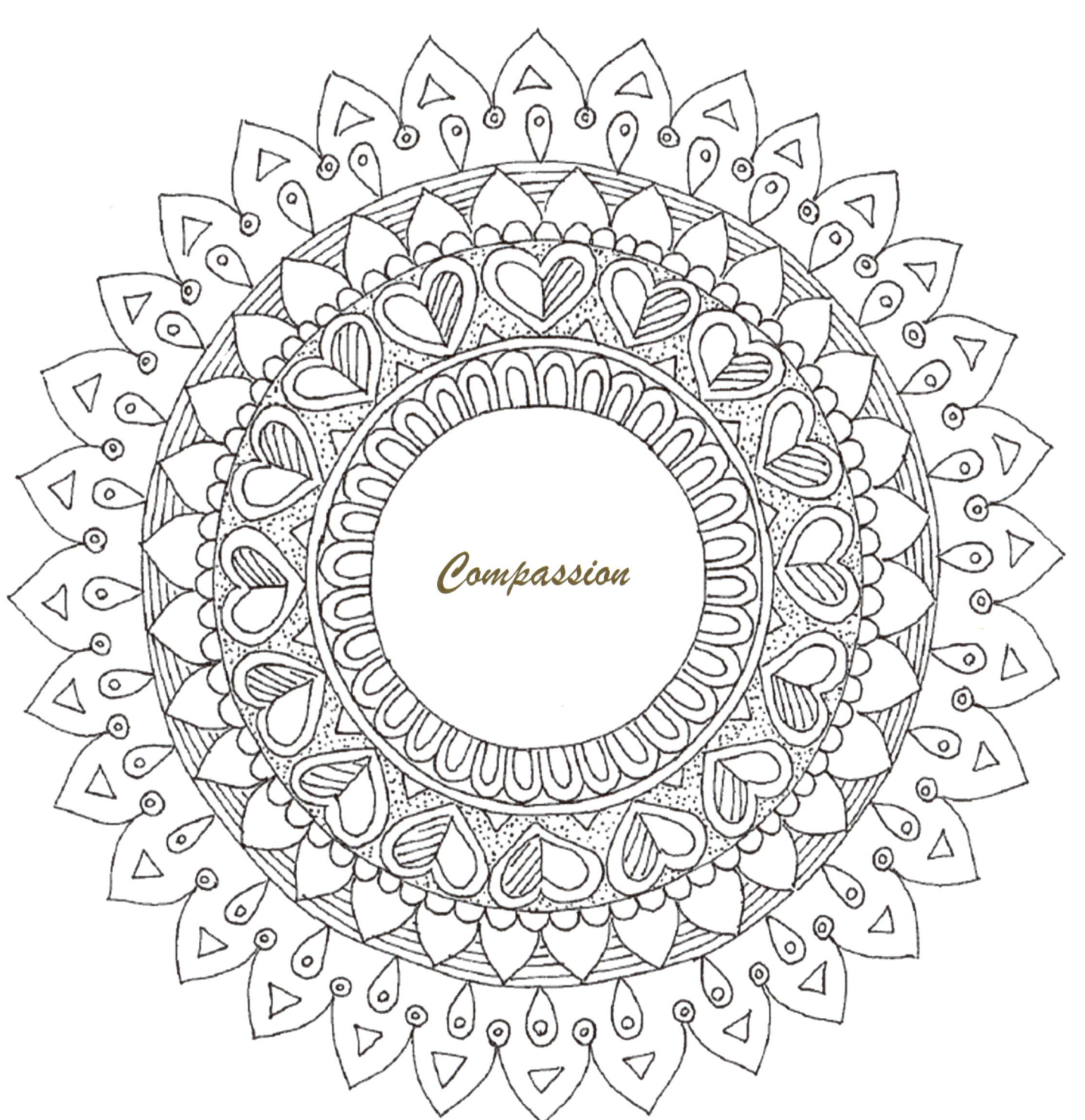

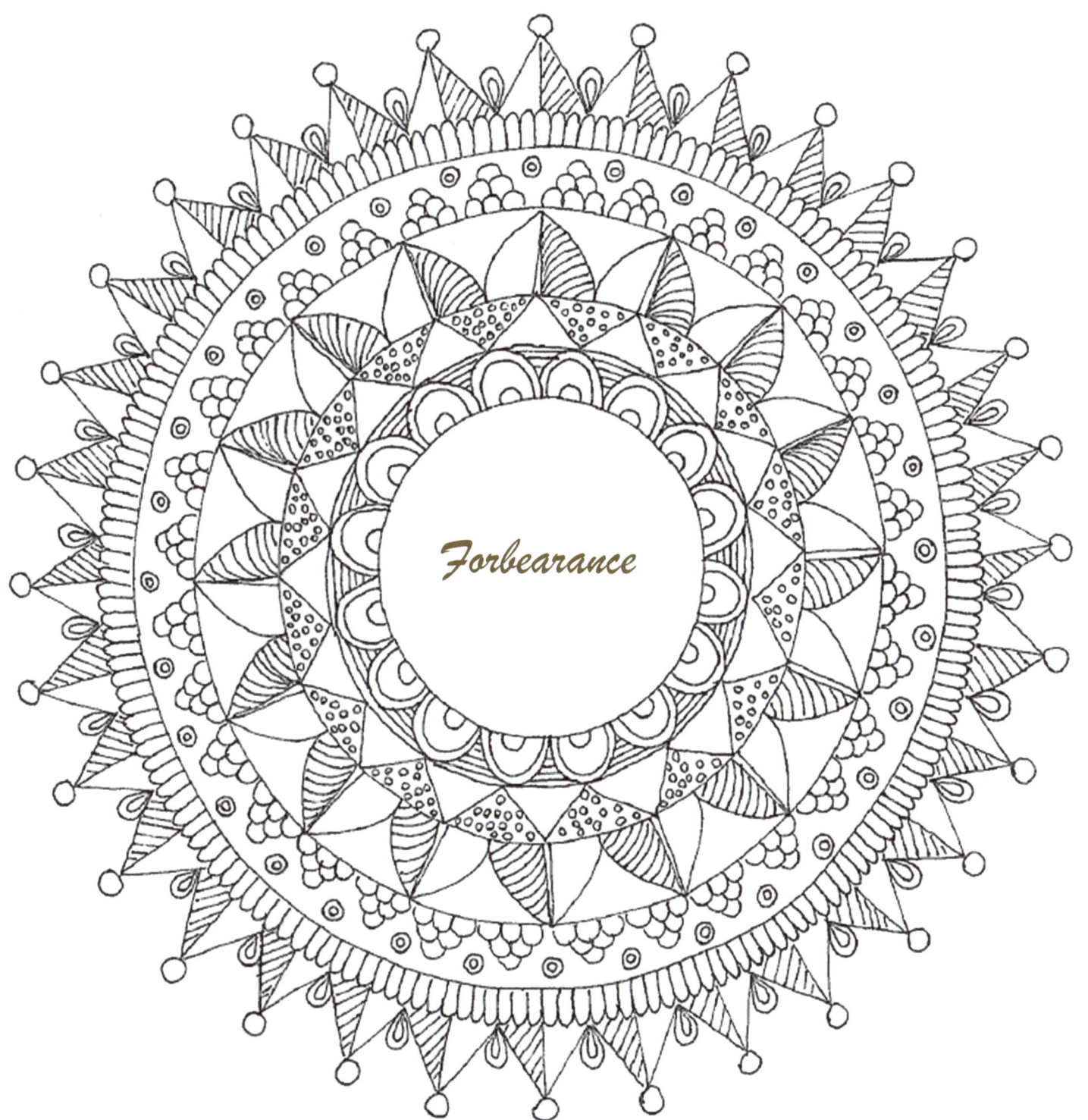

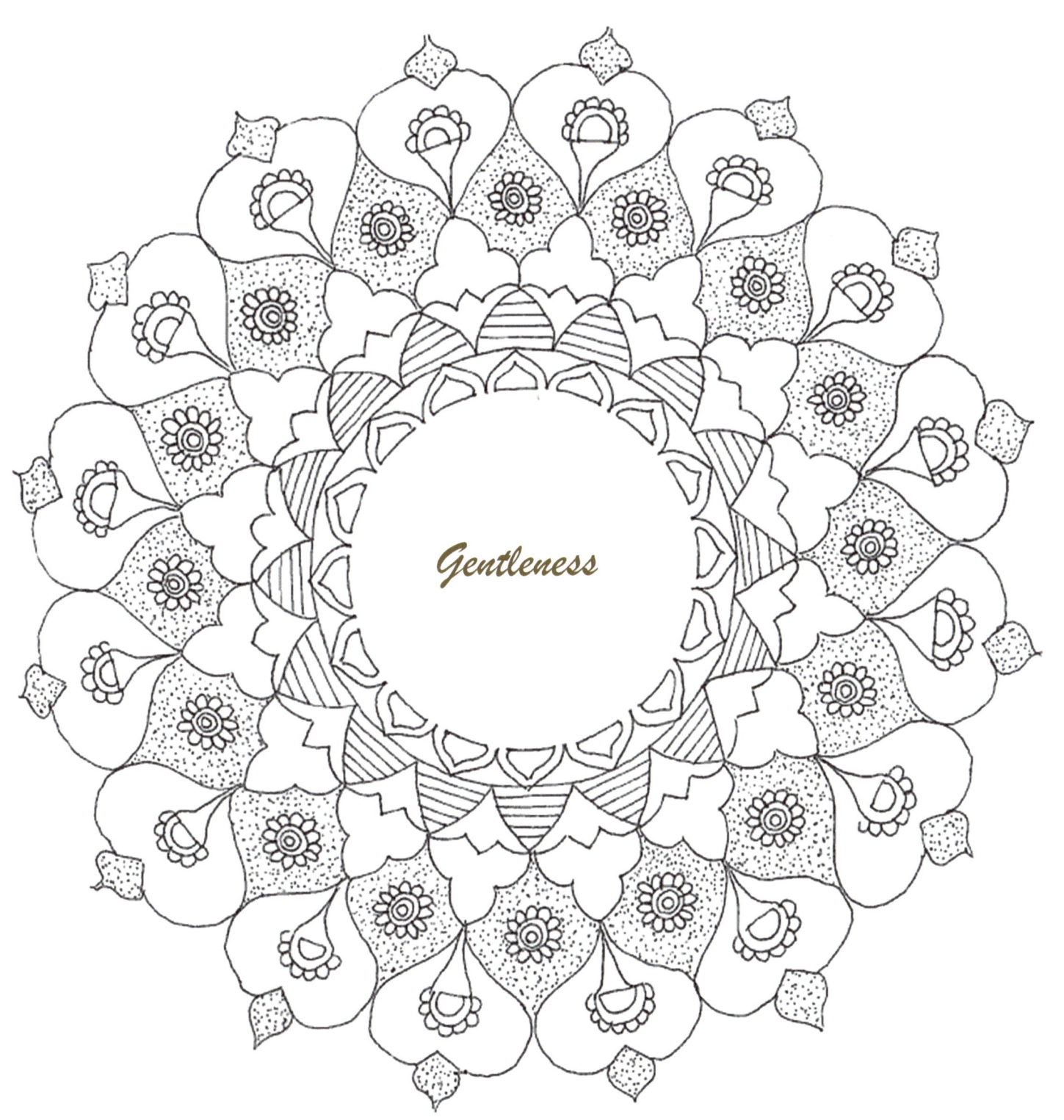

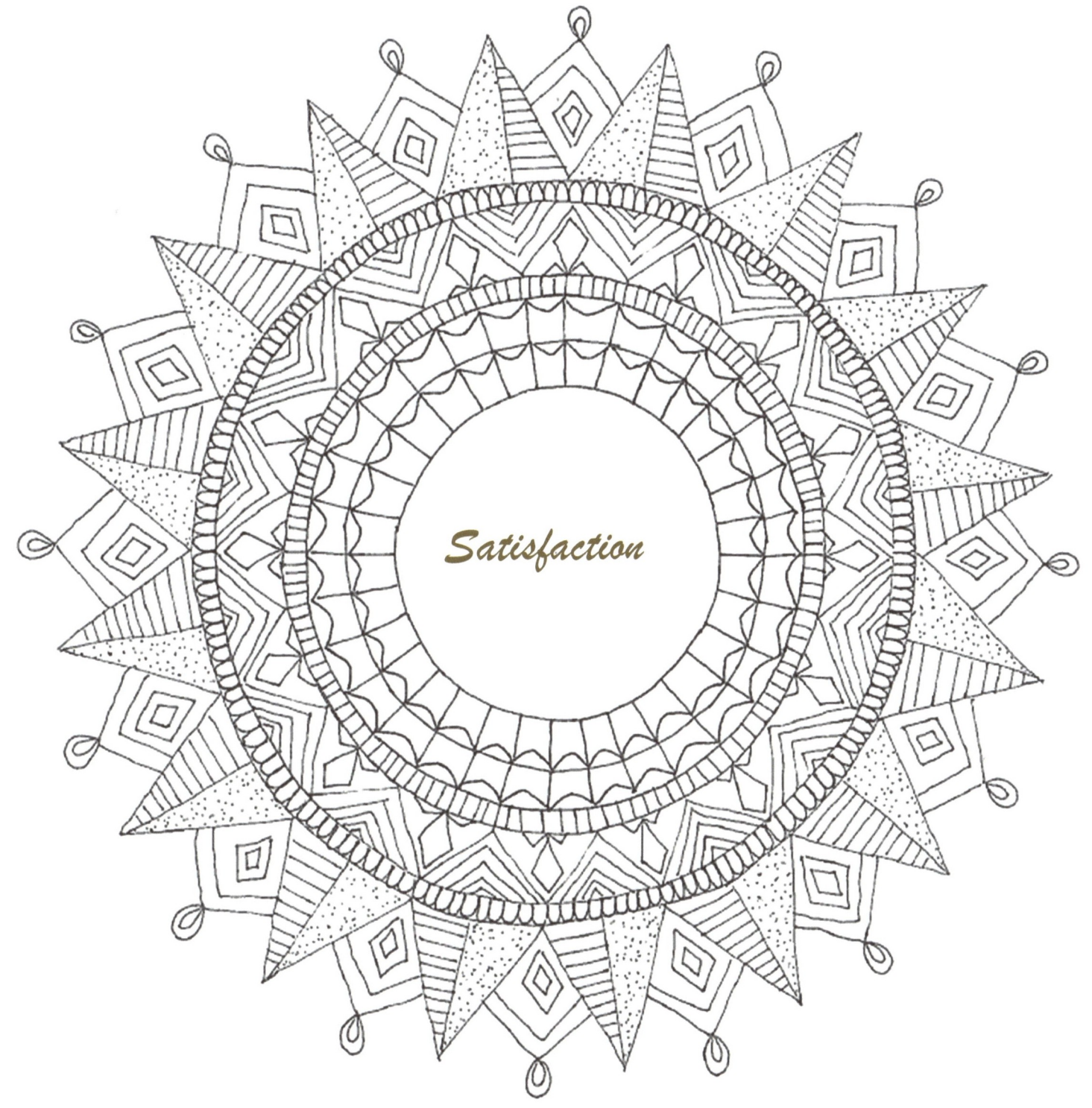

Sample Coloured Mandala - 1

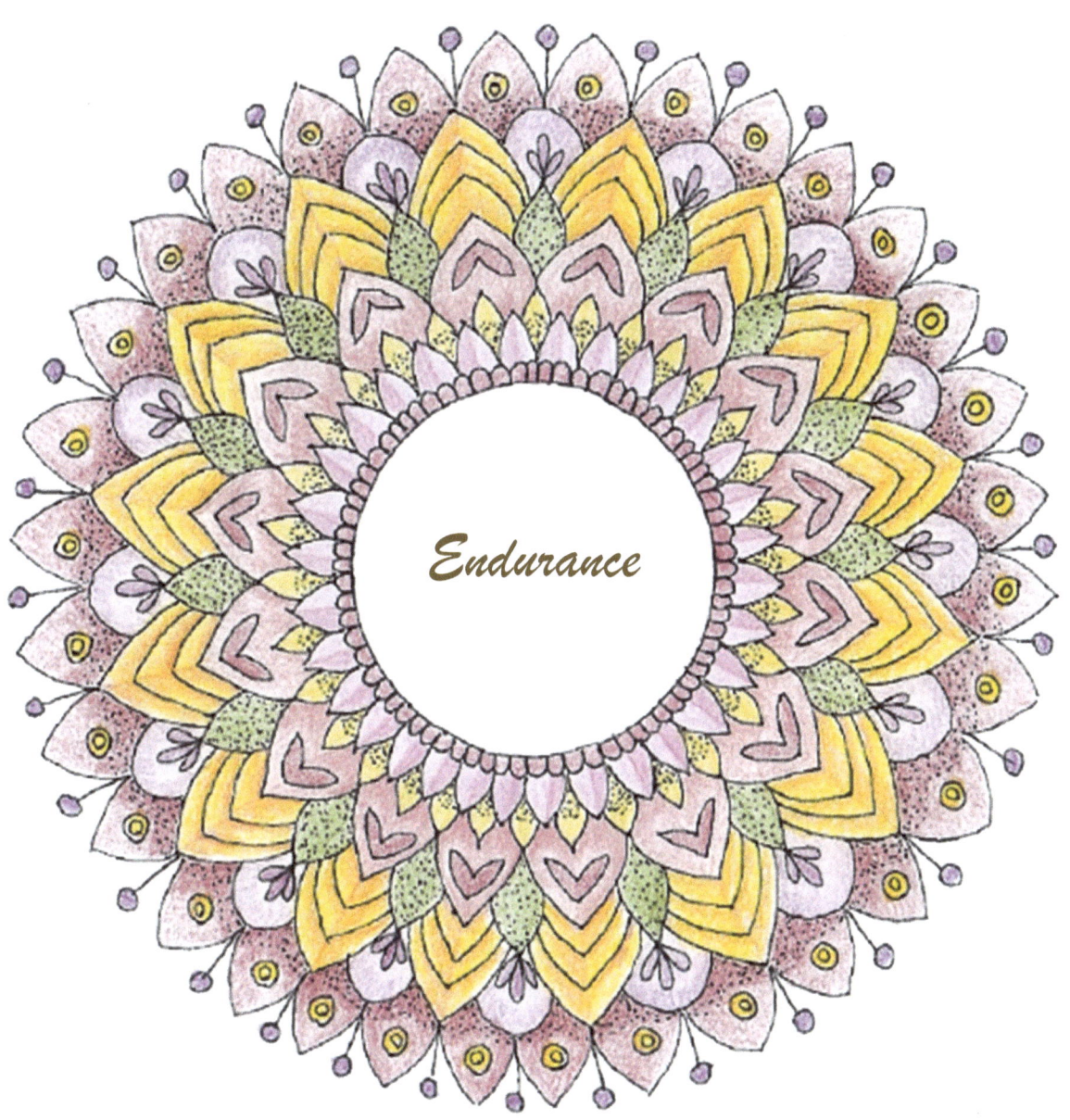

Sample Coloured Mandala - 2

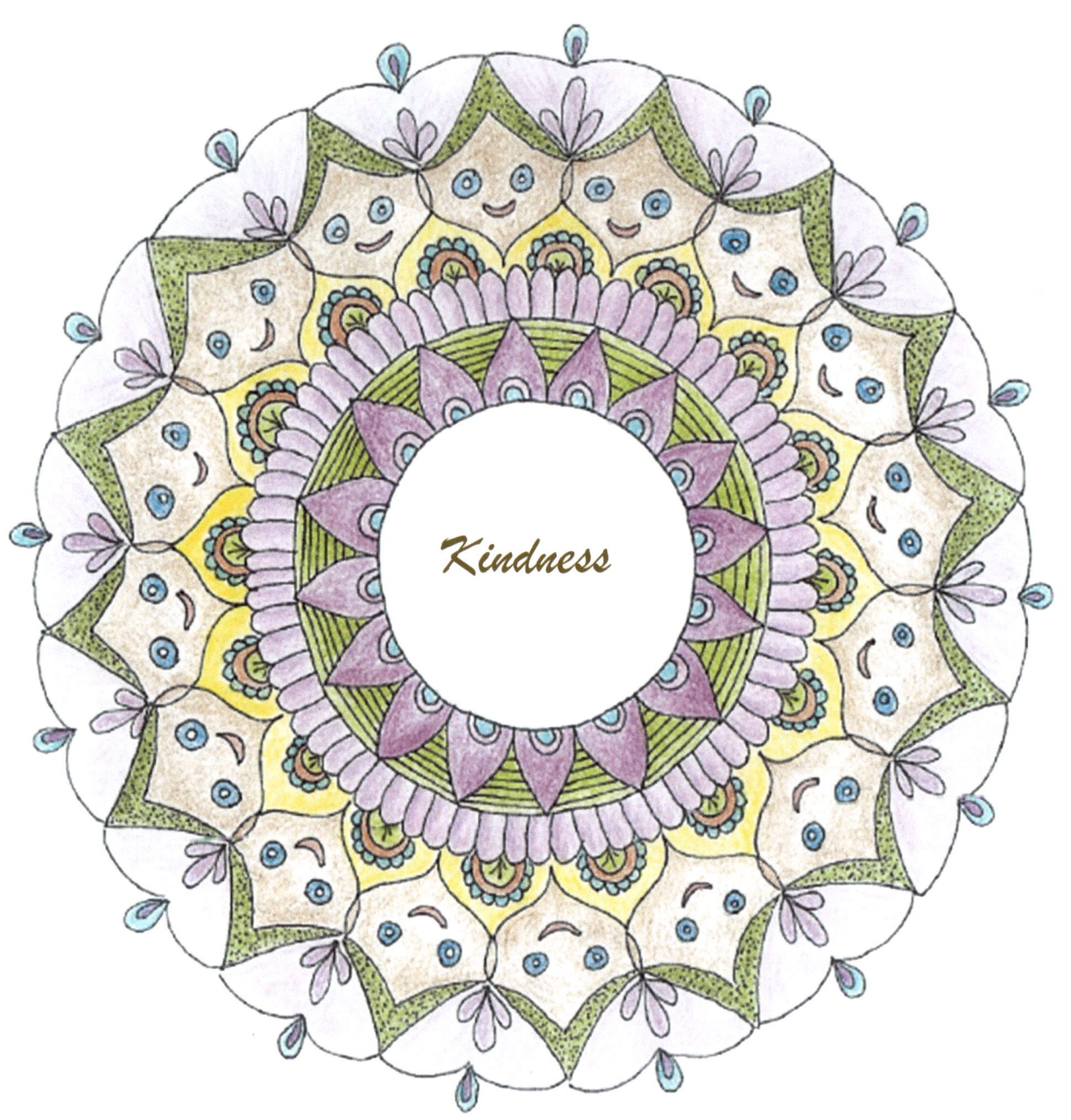

Sample Coloured Mandala - 3

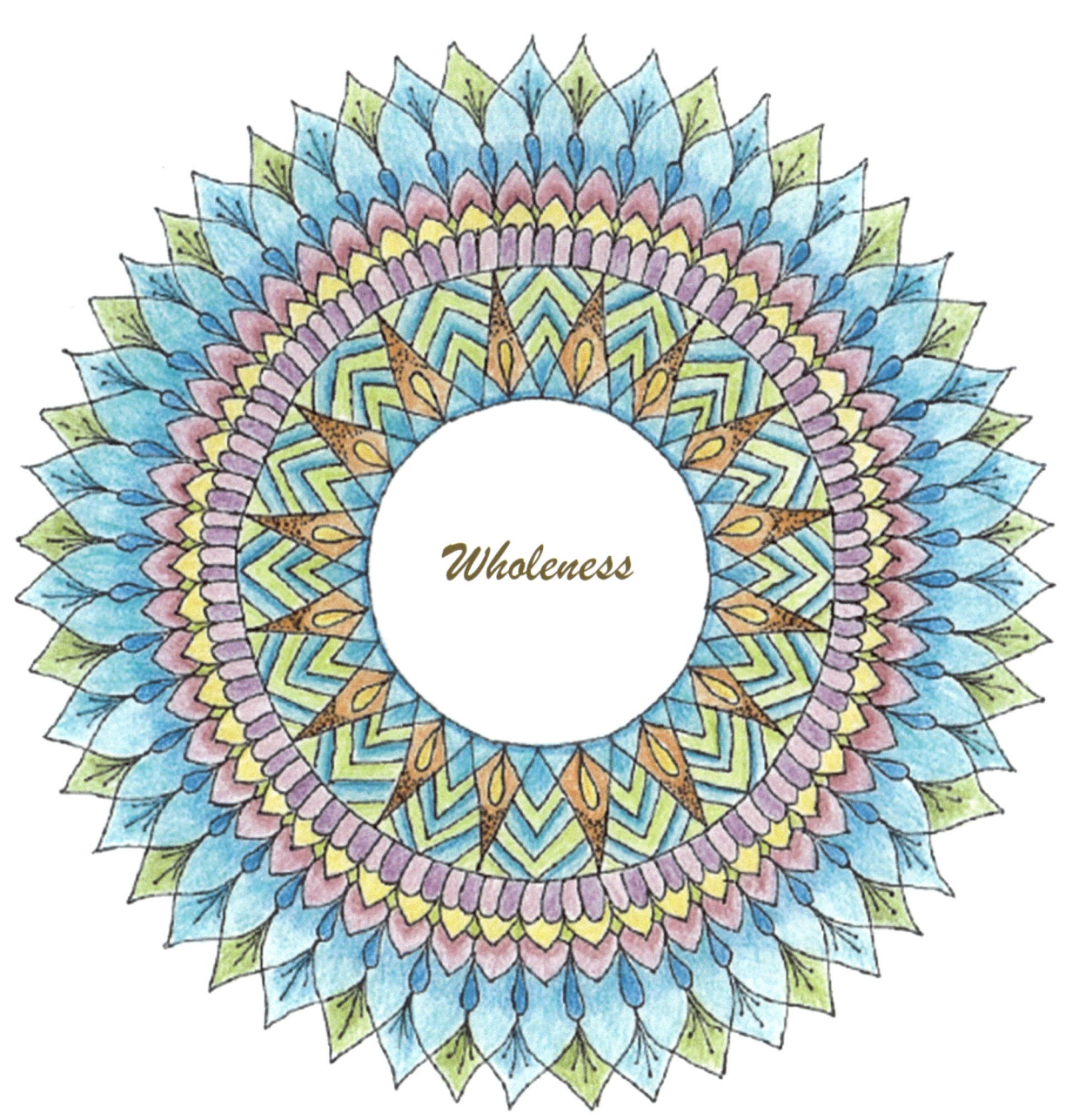

Sample Coloured Mandala - 4

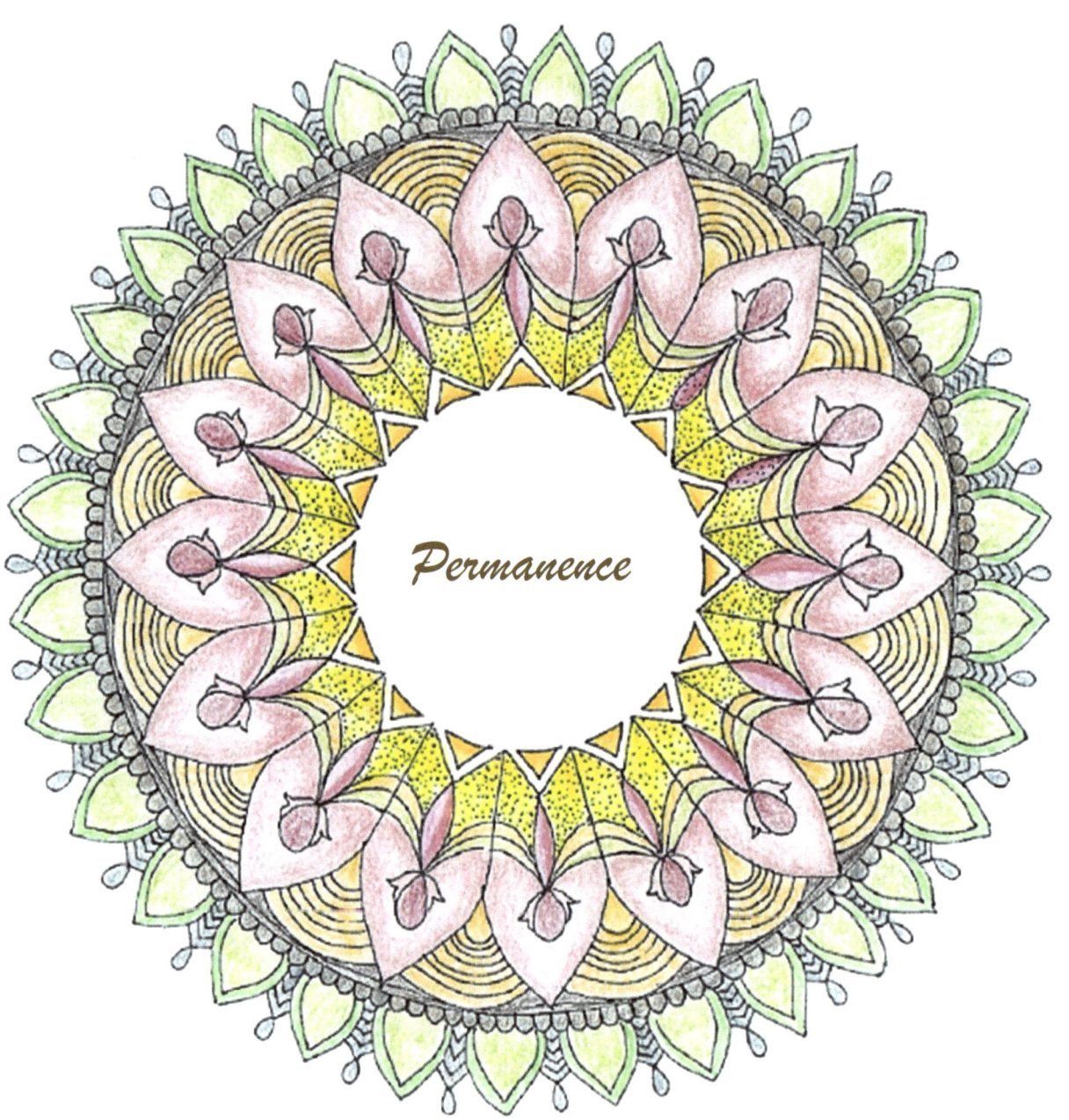

Sample Coloured Mandala - 5

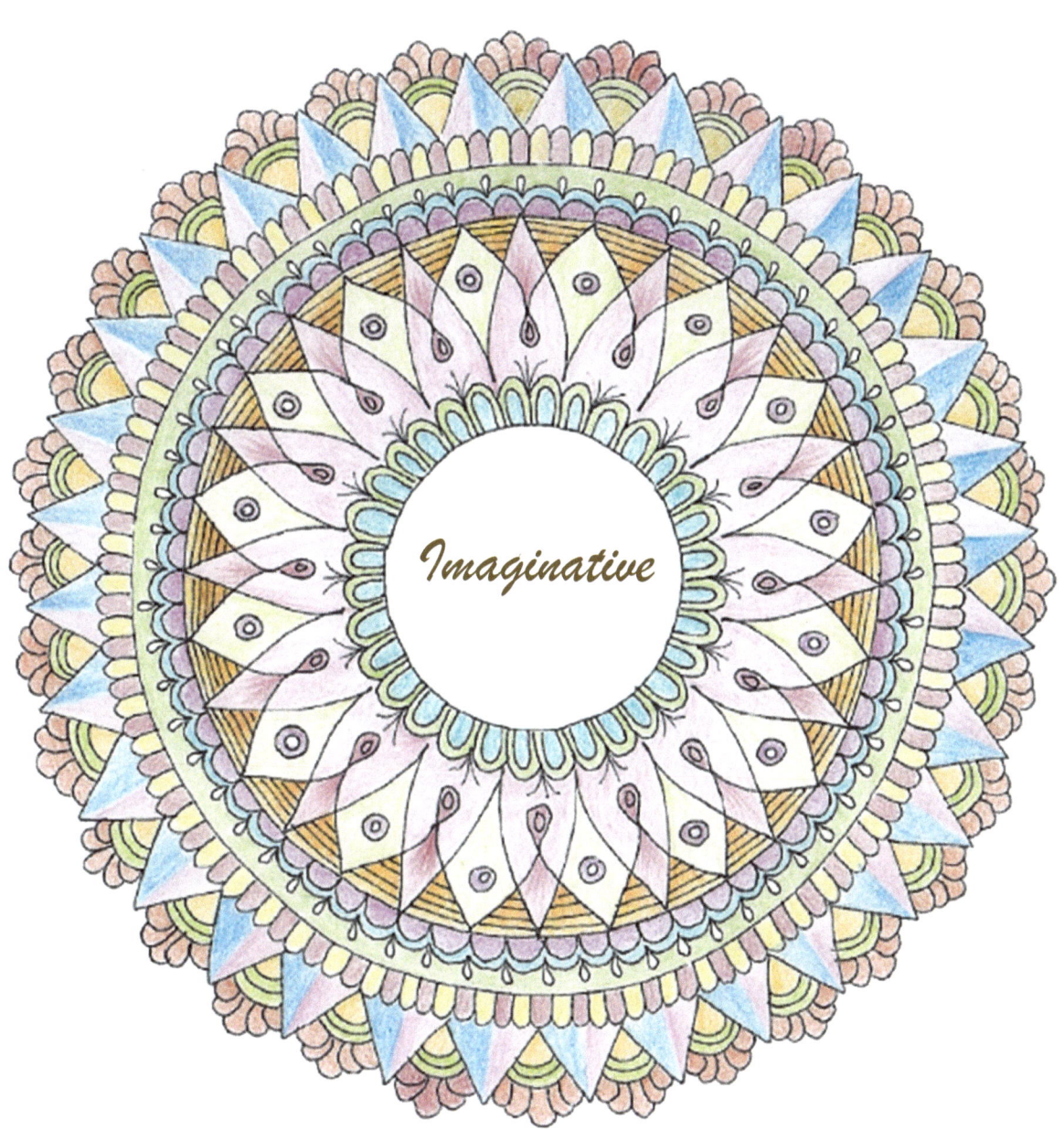

www.ingramcontent.com/pod-product-compliance
Lightning Source LLC
Chambersburg PA
CBHW051211220526
45473CB00003B/994